For my Mother and Father

CONTENTS

1 INTRODUCTION

When we, Constantine Augustus and Licinius Augustus, met so happily at Milan, and considered together all that concerned the interest and security of the State, we decided . . . to grant to Christians and to everybody the free power to follow the religion of their choice, in order that all that is divine in the heavens may be favorable and propitious towards us and towards all who are placed under our authority.

11

— from a rescript issued at Nicomedia by Licinius, June 13, 313.[1]

There have been few if any moments in history as dramatic as that which occurred at the beginning of the fourth century when an oppressed but inspired minority found itself instantly released into a career of great promise. Imperial patrons and traditions were suddenly, surprisingly, allied with the Church in an effort to do nothing less than rehabilitate ancient Mediterranean civilization. This remarkable compact, to which much early Christian art bears eloquent testimony, sought to endow life with meaning and values which the aging Roman imperial establishment alone could no longer provide; and for those objectives a cognate visual and spatial setting was required. There had been little Christian building before 313,[2] but a new architecture appeared almost immediately afterward, an architecture which has significantly enriched human experience. Its purpose was to express the belief and house the celebrations of those for whom the Incarnation and the Atonement were the very substance and meaning of the universe.

The first Christian architects set out to compose spaces which imitated and intimated that universe in both transcendent and symbolic terms. In churches, memorials, and shrines they sought to capture and expound the central convictions of faith, and that quest set Christian architecture apart from the architecture of the past. Not only were congregations given places for assembly and worship; more important, the buildings scaled down and made viable the abstract immensity of the fundamentals declared by the new religion, and each visual element, whether decorative or more purely architectural, was played to that end. During the fourth and fifth centuries, as dogma and liturgy were given authoritative form, dispositions of shapes and spaces were created which prefigured nearly the entire repertory of Christian building. The majestic architecture of the Greco-Roman world was succeeded by an architecture which proposed an entirely different purpose and meaning. Yet early Christian and Byzantine architecture inevitably evolved many forms, visual effects, and structural solutions from those already in existence, and it can be comprehended only if that background is taken into consideration.[3]

As the State hoped for the efficacy of the support of the Church, so the Church sought to make use of the established and familiar net of government; if each at times tried most energetically to change the ways of the other, this did not sunder their close and indeed necessary liaison. The Church, the Christianity of men and institutions, came of age in the world of the Late Roman Empire, to which it was inextricably tied. That world was a curious amalgam of sophistication and barbarity. It was at once weary and energetic, stultified and creative. Through much of its fabric, its currents and forces were at cross-purposes and not the least of the objectives of the Church was to unite and redirect those forces with a fresh view and will.

The new faith spread most rapidly in the Hellenistic east and in Italy, and in those lands the first monumental Christian architecture appeared (plate 1). From them it radiated, meeting and coalescing with varied local solutions. Almost all this architecture was collaterally related, having a common source in the architecture of the last two centuries of the pre-Christian Empire. A superbly creative style, in sharp contrast to the many clouded and uncertain aspects of the world in which it stood, that late Roman architecture was one of the prime achievements of ancient society; in it a major part of the formal patterns of Christian architecture can be discerned.

In the widest view Roman imperial architecture, in its ultimate function an experience of the direction and control of human purpose by interior spaces, was expressed in two distinct and nearly antithetical fashions: longitudinally and vertically. Combinations of these were common enough, but rather mechanical and hardly organized. The creative junction and interpenetration of horizontal axes with centralized vaulted shapes was to be one of the major achievements of Byzantine architecture.

In Roman designs the two elements are clearly separable if not always discrete; both shaped public and private life and ceremony by means of their ordered, compelling spaces.⁴ They resulted from a long period of interaction among Hellenistic, Near Eastern, and Latin influences, during which the elements of architecture—program, plan, structure, shape, and effect—were repeatedly investigated and redefined. Roman architects concentrated both upon planar, prismatic basilican spaces of essentially horizontal direction, and upon plastic vaulted spaces expanded from central vertical lines. From the former they freely extracted elements such as screens of columns or decorative entablatures and attached them to the latter, and they frequently juxtaposed basilican and vaulted designs.[5]

Both expressions were taken up by the Christian architect, and it is possible to make rough divisions between them according to use and geography. Generally speaking, the basilican building, with its clearly defined hall set along a primary horizontal axis, was the usual form for congregational purposes in the Latin West, centralized and vaulted structures being reserved chiefly for baptismal, memorial, and mortuary purposes. In the East, though the basilican form was popular in the fourth and fifth centuries, it was substantially replaced by ingenious vaulted buildings whose spatial and visual complexities were the result of an interest in combining and interconnecting the simpler vaulted units of the past.

Tradition and novelty were combined in about equal parts in the new Christian basilica of the fourth century. The basic form had long since been in civil use in the Greco-Roman world and was a symbol of authority and social order. It had many applications in markets, town halls (plate 2), throne rooms (plate 3) and cult buildings (plate 4); in all these the lucid underlying visual and physical structure of the basilica prevailed, even if there were differences of scale, proportion, or the disposition of openings. That underlying structure was of two or four long parallel files of columns, occasionally of piers, surrounded by an outer wall at an aisle's distance. The central, widest space, or nave, was usually heightened by thin sheets of clerestory walls, with a beam or simple truss roof of timber, in section an isosceles triangle of fairly low altitude, crossing the span. Low-pitched roofs covered the flanking aisles at a lesser height.

The principal entrance might be at the center of one of the long sides, the aisles might return around the whole plan, one or both of the shorter sides might be closed by a curving wall, or cult and throne rooms might be roofed by single longitudinal barrel vaults; but irrespective of these variations, the basic axial and therefore basilican focus remained constant. Parts and spaces were clearly stated, self-evident. The central nave, its roof timbering usually hidden by a flat ceiling, was a spacious rectangular shaft laid on its side, visually reinforced in its directional command by aisles running alongside. The files of columns, dividing the building into major and subsidiary spatial strips, measured with their regular meter one's progress along the path prescribed. The lines of column bases, of capitals and imposts, and the stretched entablatures or even, rhythmic, superposed arcades, outlined perspective boxes in powerful orthogonals operative from any position on the paving (plate 5).

The whole was stated in quite simple structural terms; it was fairly easy to build, yet could be expanded to a nave width of seventy or even eighty feet; but it was not fireproof, and it had no vertical monumentality. The basilica did, however, have great dignity and simplicity and close connotations of legal and social authority, and it made possible huge congregational and ceremonial halls. Most important of all, with its main entrance in one of the shorter sides, it had driving point and focus: with elemental directness and power the controlling lines and forces bore upon a distant end wall.

The vaulted centralized buildings were more complex and precocious. Essentially they were developed from a common interest, in both the East and West, in signaling architecturally the significance of a single place or experience, in making tombs, shrines, and canopied enframements for gods or rulers. The motives and resources of the Roman State played upon these interests with great vigor, and from the first century A.D. onward a sequence of remarkable buildings, chiefly secular, appeared in this mode. Increasingly ingenious solutions of vaulting problems helped to make possible a repertory of forms and spaces having in common the qualities of envelopment and enframement under a single curving feature.

Roman technological capacities increased the size and complexity of these buildings through the use of concrete and brick, relatively plastic materials which not only simplified the problems of forming curved surfaces but also allowed the architects to channel the thrusts of superstructures out and down to the ground along all but hidden lines. Such buildings as the vestibule

15

and nymphaeum of the Piazza d'Oro of Hadrian's Tivoli Villa or the so-called Temple of Minerva Medica in Rome (plates 6 and 7) made their chief interior effect as seemingly light and airy pavilions, enveloping the viewer in spaces of vertical accent wherein the relationship between the vaulted cover and its supports was not readily seen.[6]

In the development of this style the vertical supports gradually became less bulky and the walls ceased to function either structurally or visually as load-bearing. In some cases the walls all but disappeared, and the vertical elements formed pierced, almost skeletal frames carrying vaults above. These structures were of square, circular, or polygonal plan, with a vault or tent-shaped roof of timber resting on piers or columns disposed about a central vertical axis. In contrast to the horizontal basilican form, they made a presence about a specific spot, and while in the process of development and experiment, passed into the world of Christian architecture.

These enveloping, seamless vaulted forms were peculiarly suited to Christian memorials, baptisteries, and shrines. They traced revolving imitations of the cosmos with expanses of modeled surfaces so fluidly interconnected as to conjure away their material reality. They stated direct lines of force and connection from centered, hallowed ceremonial spots below to made heavens above. But they did not describe adequate ceremonial spaces and lacked processional axes, and thus for a while stood apart from the basilican halls. Yet their symbolic significance and their memorial associations were so important that ways were sought to combine them with congregational and processional buildings, and in early Christian architecture a number of attempts were made to marry the horizontal shed with the verticalized pavilion.[7] Apses and sanctuaries were lengthened in order to pull horizontal axes under and past the vertical axes of vaulted, centralized buildings (plate 39), pavilion units were inserted into basilicas (plate 26), and cross forms of various kinds were tried (plates 20 and 34); ultimately, the problem was solved in Hagia Sophia (plates 54 and 55).

The willingness of the first Christian architects directly to adapt previous forms should not be taken to mean that their architecture was merely derivative. That they did make ample use of Greco-Roman architecture was the result of the sudden prominence of the Church and perhaps of the authority of an imperial office of works.[8] They had no substantial precedents of their own to follow. What is perhaps surprising is the great extent to which they were creative and original on such short notice. Their monumental churches succeeded brilliantly in marking for a rapidly changing world the essence of the newly freed faith, and they set forth profoundly efficacious solutions to the problems posed for architecture by that faith. These solutions were comparable to those found in the figure arts, where Christian artists continued the lines of development of late antique style but informed it with a radically different content and meaning. This process was aided to a certain extent by the increasing divinization of the autocrat and the orientalization of the mood and structure of the State.[9] But Christian architecture nevertheless emerged as a style with governing principles clearly independent of those of the basic pre-Christian architectural directions sketched above. Both liturgy–with its requisite setting and furnishings (plate 8)–and illustration–treating the central story of the Church chiefly in mosaic–came into play together with less immediately tangible elements.

The architectural vocabulary of the past was, so to speak, disassembled, and its parts, though often still recognizable, were reconsidered and regrouped. The orders of peristylar temples and of stoas were brought indoors and disposed in symbolic plans. The great secular vaults of the Romans became the all but invisible supports for interior sheaths of paradisiacal color. Interior surfaces, treated with abstract simplicity, were rendered insubstantial and were subordinated to the symbolic, intimating spaces which became the reality of the architecture. In all this light was a prime ingredient, so channeled and manipulated as to increase the effects of mysteriousness and immateriality. Before the time of the first Constantine these principles had been explored tentatively if at all; during the second half of his reign they defined the first Christian architecture.

17

2   EARLY CHRISTIAN ARCHITECTURE

Constantine's effect upon the world was remarkable. He removed the seat of government from Rome to Byzantium, made
Christianity licit, and not only openly allied himself with the
Church, but assumed within it an anomalous but authoritative
station.[10] He was not of its hierarchy except by his own assumption, but that assumption was based upon the solid ground of
his secular and financial means. He provided for great church
buildings, and he energetically assisted the episcopacy in its
search for a clear and precise declaration of faith. He was a
revolutionary by any definition, a *turbator rerum*, as his contemporaries realized, yet a despot of pre-Christian inspiration.[11]
An extraordinary product of a thoroughly extraordinary age,

Constantine, whose private religious convictions remain enigmatic, assisted in creating dogma and architecture for Christianity.

Monumental churches, chiefly in Palestine and Rome, resulted from this portentous imperial association. Constantine's architects—their names and careers are almost entirely unrecorded—creatively enframed the already well-established liturgy, and so effected the passage from late antique to early Christian style. Their immediate objectives were the housing of congregations, a sufficient monumentality, a suitable focus upon venerated locations or relics, and a disposition of forms and spaces proper for the iterated ceremonies which recalled and celebrated the generative events of three centuries past. They created buildings of basilican form intended above all as settings for the Eucharist; but at the same time centralized, more purely memorial structures were erected that might house the Eucharist but were used primarily to mark and enshrine places or objects associated with Gospel episodes or other hallowed events.

The results were seen at an early date in Palestine, where, under Constantine's orders, churches were built at the sites of the Nativity and the Entombment. Both buildings have been drastically altered since their foundation, but their general forms have been recovered by combining the study of the remaining original portions with evidence from early descriptions and generalized pictorial representations.[12] Their association with the most sacred of all Christian localities and their early date (both were probably begun about 326) ensured their direct influence upon the future of church architecture.

The architect Zenobius aligned the several parts of the Holy Sepulchre in an alternating sequence of open and closed spaces (plate 9). From the eastern entrance off a market place one passed into a columned atrium court, and from that into a five-aisled basilica of square plan. Lit by a clerestory, sheathed in colored marbles, and crowned by flat, gilded ceilings, the basilica was finished by a transept and an apse or shrine flanked by openings leading out into the court of Calvary.[13] West of that court stood the slightly later rotunda of the Anastasis, a hundred feet in diameter, which enclosed the tomb of Christ in tiered concentric rings of space capped by a dome (plate 10).

Almost all the elements of the early Christian style were thus lucidly exposed. Each purposeful part—the atrium for catechumens and visitors, the basilica for the congregational Eucharist, and the shrine-form of the Anastasis rotunda—remained independent in a rather Roman fashion, but a whole was created by the rhythmic sequence of light and less light and the repetition of carefully disposed emotional and architectural climaxes. Behind the basic organization of the plan lay a normal Roman usage in houses and palaces, a progression from the more public to the more private.[14] At the Sepulchre that usage was translated into spiritual and hierarchical terms, shaping an architectural interpretation of a reality beyond human knowledge. However influential more practical aspects such as communications, topography, and construction might remain, the central directive of the new architecture was overridingly spiritual.

At Bethlehem the Church of the Nativity, a somewhat smaller building, made use of the same elements as the Sepulchre but in it they are pulled tightly together (plate 11).[15] Presumably a more or less square atrium, walled in and on axis, stood before the basilica proper; the latter, also square in plan, had five aisles but no transept. Directly at the far end of the basilica and opening from it was an octagonal form set over the grotto of the Nativity. The octagon, two-thirds as wide as the basilica, marked, like the Anastasis in Jerusalem, a sacred spot; it also provided for a circulating traffic of visitors and pilgrims. It was probably covered with a pyramidal wooden roof centering over the observation pit and grille below. Both the Church of the Nativity and the Sepulchre showed the results of keen interest in practical problems connected with the display and veneration of sacred sites; both marked and emphasized those sites with centered memorial forms; both associated those forms with compacted basilicas.

Tradition, and Constantine's desire to do something magnificent for the capital he was about to abandon, may in part explain the immense scale of his churches of S. Peter and S. John

Lateran in Rome. The Lateran, the earlier of the two and probably the first of all monumental churches, was an elongated five-aisled basilica, almost certainly without a transept, but culminating in a generous apse well scaled to the three-hundred-foot sweep of the nave and aisles. It was not primarily a memorial building or shrine, but rather the church of the bishop, who then resided at the Lateran, and thus of the city of Rome.

Old S. Peter's, on the other hand, was not only a congregational church but a memorial shrine as well, built upon the traditional site of the apostle's tomb (plates 12 and 13). A basilica on the scale of the Lateran, it was fitted with an immense transept (about fifty by three hundred feet) which in plan might seem to have barred the processional axis and longitudinal view from the basilica proper.[16] In practice, however, these functions were not at all obviated by the transept; the controlling lines and views from the nave passed unbroken to the shrine enframed by the distant apse. Also, the original main altar of S. Peter's was presumably placed in the transept, perhaps near the triumphal arch over the opening between nave and transept; the sanctuary was reserved for the canopied shrine and tomb. By shifting the building's structural axis and thus suppressing for a space the longitudinal files of columns, the transept facilitated circulation, and by crossing the major spatial axis of the building, it assisted both symbolically and visually in fixing and marking the capital feature of the whole.

This desire and necessity to center, focus, and celebrate architecturally a specific feature or space is an outstanding characteristic of Christian architecture. Constantine's designers experimented with axial emphasis, crossed longitudinal and transeptal axes, rotundas, and octagons. A variation can be seen in S. Costanza in Rome (plates 14–16).[17] Possibly intended as a mausoleum, this domed building owes much to the centrally planned structures of the Romans. It consists of two thick concentric rings of brick-faced concrete, the inner, higher ring resting upon coupled columns set out radially from the central vertical axis; the outer, lower ring encloses a circular ambulatory whose space flows between the columns into the axial cylinder. The effect is that of a central bright hollow hedged about by a circular screen, which is in turn embraced by a darker, more intimate corridor. All views are of necessity oblique, and two disparate worlds are created, one of immediately human scale by the ambulatory, with its complexity of curving walls, vaults, and screens; another, less finite, by the elevated central capsule lit by windows in its high drum. Formerly, all the vaults were sheathed in colored mosaics; those in the ambulatory still survive. Both the structural mechanism of the building and its piled-up hierarchy of forms prefigured the more complex, less ponderous centralized architecture to come.

Clearly there was no one basic kind of Constantinian church. Even the basilican form was variously treated and cannot be said to have been in any way standardized. Some Constantinian buildings had transepts, some did not. Galleries above the aisles appeared at the Sepulchre but not at S. Peter's. Apses were either inscribed within flat end walls or projected beyond them in curving or polygonal shapes. Centralized buildings might be composed of single or multiple space rings rising from either round or polygonal plans. But the objectives of early Christian architecture were clearly stated during the first half of the fourth century; after that, the achievements of the age of Constantine were restudied and reset.

Broadly speaking, there was less innovation in the Latin West, where the prestigious pilgrimage basilicas of Rome remained the chief architectural guide for centuries, than in the Hellenized East. There the importance of the new capital, the proximity of the most sanctified shrines, and the leavening experimental forces of Syrian, Anatolian, and Aegean architecture all encouraged a heightened creativity. There was of course interplay, sometimes of very considerable significance, between East and West, for there are experimental buildings in Italy and traditional basilicas of more or less Roman form in the East. But in general it was the aware and sensitive Greek talent of the Eastern provinces that next shaped Christian architecture.

With the exception of S. Costanza, none of the buildings of Constantine's family have been preserved other than in a frag-

23

mentary way. However, after Christianity became the official state religion at the end of the fourth century the quantity of church building increased markedly. The architecture of the later fourth century is largely unknown, but a large number of buildings of the fifth and sixth centuries stand today. During this period the general tendency was to build on a fairly small scale, with the exception of further pilgrimage churches in Rome (S. Maria Maggiore; S. Paul's Outside the Walls, plate 5), and the imperial foundations in Constantinople (the first Holy Apostles, the first and second Hagia Sophia and the other buildings of the capitol); in the provinces, where church officials and parishes usually had far smaller resources, the results were less grandiose. Church building went on almost irrespective of the military crises and dogmatic controversies which rent the civil and ecclesiastical fabric, and by the early sixth century the results were gathered in Constantinople at the beginning of a period of relative stability.

Constantinople, "this city of the world's desire," was founded by Constantine in 330 after six years' preparation and construction on the site of the old Greek town of Byzantium. Superbly located and soon to be provided with nearly impregnable defenses (plate 17), the city was stocked by Constantine with the images and customs of Rome. But inevitably the abruptness and extent of the change deeply affected ancient usages and ideas. In time Constantinople became the center of the Byzantine world—culturally Greek, juridically Roman, officially and passionately Christian.[18] Meanwhile the architecture of the neighboring provinces underwent a complementary transition, in which the strongest motivation was to fuse centralized with longitudinal, memorial with processional, forms. The major developments were as follows.

In southern Syria the drive toward centralization had been apparent in a number of stone and timber temples and headquarters buildings of the Roman period, for example in the second-century *praetorium* at Musmiyeh, the ancient Phaena, a square building extended by an inscribed apse and side chambers (plates 18 and 19). Two or three centuries later it was converted to Christian use by the addition of four interior columns to form a square pavilion, with a concrete cloister vault; from that square, and below the springing of the central vault, four barrel vaults of stone slabs extended to the outer walls. A clearly articulated volumetric cross was formed, spatially accented and pinned by the higher middle feature, a rectangular relative of S. Costanza in Rome. The Church of the Prophets, Apostles and Martyrs at Gerasa, dedicated in 464, was an unvaulted development of this idea (plate 23). There the arms of the cross, about thirty feet in span, were defined by short colonnades, outlining a processional axis intersected by a centered transept; rising from the intersection, presumably, was a square stone tower roofed pyramidally in wood.[19]

At about the same time, work was begun in northern Syria upon the multiple church of S. Simeon, an ascetic pillar-saint of great fame and influence (plates 20–22). There four three-aisled basilicas were engaged to alternating sides of a central octagon which rose above the converging basilican ridge-lines and was lit by large clerestory windows. The naves focused and opened upon the central room while the aisles intercommunicated through splayed chambers of trapezoidal plan. The effect was of expansion to great scale of the Gerasa church, though without the circumscribing wall. Plastically, the parts were disparate, artificially assembled; functionally and visually, they were coherent.

In 513, at the Cathedral of Bosra in the south, a major experiment was made in centralized design (plate 24). A huge circle, some one hundred and twenty feet in diameter, was encased within a rectangular niched exterior. A square tower on angle piers was placed within the circle, expanding columnar exedrae stood between the piers, and a deep sanctuary and apse suggested a longitudinal, horizontal accent. Complicated volumes and interrupted vistas resulted, enhanced by the restless, undulating surfaces of the interior wall. Spatially, Bosra clearly pointed toward the Byzantine style, while retaining Syrian characteristics of exterior rectangularity, massive framing, and jarring interior transitions from part to part.

But the basilican form also flourished in Syria, as the arms of S. Simeon show. Usually of splendidly precise stonework, sometimes with powerful transverse diaphragm arches supporting their timber superstructures, these Syrian longitudinal churches often were surprisingly Romanesque in effect. The monastery church of Der Turmanin, probably of the sixth century, was composed of ruggedly massive blocklike units (plate 25). These were piled up in a two-tower façade with arched central motives. The nave and aisles terminated in an apse flanked by extended side chambers (used for robing and liturgical preparations) in the manner of Bosra.[20] In all these Syrian buildings the detailing was essentially late classical in mood, of shallow relief, and was used in running strips which helped visually to tie together the major architectural and spatial elements.

The heavy, boxy effects of the Syrian buildings were less evident closer to Constantinople. At Alahan Kilise in Cilicia, probably of the late fifth or early sixth century, a square tower was set into a longitudinal building (plate 26). Less massive solids and the use of subordinated column screens to flank the crossing helped to create a more subtle design in which Syrian and Aegean influences were combined. Within Anatolia proper Syrian ideas flourished, but around the Aegean Roman methods were combined with theatrical Hellenistic forms to produce a more supple, flowing architecture. In Syria the variety of effects had been rather limited by the extremely hard local stones and the narrow range of shapes that could be made with timber; in Salonica and the ancient Greek cities along the western coast of Asia Minor, which flourished under Roman rule, brick and concrete were available and well known.[21]

This technological difference was not definitive, but it did make possible near Constantinople the architectural expression of the geometries and volumes investigated by the post-classical Greek mind. In addition to this, Roman builders and workmen were brought from Italy to the Aegean area from the early third century onward. There is ample evidence of their work and influence, as at the rotunda of the Emperor Galerius in Salonica (later the church of S. George; plate 27), the constructions of

Septimius Severus and later emperors at Byzantium-Constantinople, and a number of secular structures in Asia Minor.[22] As in Syria, the basilica continued to be built, and it was produced in fifth-century variants such as S. Demetrius in Salonica, which perhaps had aisles continuing around its transept (plate 28, as rebuilt), and S. John of the Studion in Constantinople, with its exquisite proportions, lateral porch or narthex, and blind nave without a clerestory (plates 29 and 30).

In the West, the Christian style was expanded from central Italy at a rapid pace. The basilicas, baptistries, and chapels built in the Latin-speaking provinces were usually of that Italian inspiration which evolved from the mixing of Mediterranean ideas and forms within the late imperial scheme. One direction was characterized by the powerfully abstract aesthetic of basilicas such as S. Sabina in Rome of 422–432 (plate 31), with its unornamented, planar exterior evolved from designs of about a century before (the civil basilica at Trier; the Senate House at Rome). Inside, the sheer walls, the polished and highly reflective marble surfaces of the spandrels and paving, and the unornamented soffits of the nave arcade created an equally lucid and simplified world; in such a setting it is no surprise that round and even relief sculpture found little place (plate 32). The relative ethereality of S. Sabina contrasts with the more plastic, coloristic forms of S. Apollinare Nuovo in Ravenna of the very late fifth century (plate 33). There unfluted nave columns carried incipiently medieval capitals and robust impost blocks, and the soffits of the superposed arcades were coffered. A vast cycle of Biblical scenes and processions of martyrs in colored glass mosaic, begun by the Ostrogoths and finished under Justinian, enriched and enlivened the quintessential forms.

In the fifth century centralized and vaulted pavilion forms also appeared in Italy. Their formal genealogy can be traced to concepts expressed in the early fourth-century "Temple of Minerva Medica" in Rome (plates 6 and 7), and to influences from the East as well, but their primary meaning was symbolic and visual.[23] The straightforward exterior of the so-called Mausoleum of Galla Placidia in Ravenna, probably dating from the middle

27

of the century, with its plain brick surfaces, repeated cubical shapes, and simple lines of blank arcading, belies the extraordinary nature of its interior (plate 34).

This the architect obviously intended; exterior effects were being increasingly subdued and played down in order to awe the beholder and effectively translate his emotions when he stepped from the familiar world into the unannounced beauty and mystery of the spiritual house. These interiors defy the camera. At Galla Placidia it is an intimate, dimly lit four-armed room glowing with the subdued color of mosaics and tinted marble revetments that physically line but visually obliterate the actual substance of the building. Barrel vaults and a pendentive dome join the vertical planes of the walls in a mysterious envelope like that of the nearby contemporary Baptistry of the Orthodox (plates 35 and 36).

In the latter building an octagonal shell was magically closed to a hemispherical dome by a lacework of blank arcades and a dematerializing encrustation of color. The several horizontal registers of this transition are inhabited by a hierarchically ascending iconography of sacramentally appropriate figures and scenes. This proto-Byzantine near denial of architectural solids by a nonstructural, optically and symbolically dominant lining is one of the major achievements of Christian art. In a more purely architectural sense, the church of S. Lorenzo Maggiore in Milan, built shortly after the middle of the century, is important for the understanding of Byzantine designs (plate 37). With its congruent shells and dilating exedral spaces, it can be read as a three-dimensional expansion of the illusory interior architecture of the Orthodox Baptistry, and it is also related to two-shelled buildings east of Italy, such as an early fifth-century structure erected in Athens within Hadrian's Stoa (plate 38).[24]

Even in the face of so brief and selective a survey it would be difficult to maintain the rather common charge of decadence against the art of the Late Roman Empire. Its architects and builders met difficult and elusive problems with energy and talent, sometimes with genius. They abandoned the molding of masses for the composition of spaces. They wed their art to that of the mosaicist in an indissoluble, perfect marriage. They struck new forms, produced a new spatial vision, and created a spiritual ambient equal to any other in its capacity to move and reawaken men.

3   THE AGE OF JUSTINIAN

There is an abundance of monumental and literary evidence
for the age dominated by the objectives and personality of
Justinian. Many buildings, mosaics, and carvings of the sixth
century, nearly all formally related and of pre-eminent quality,
can be seen today around the Mediterranean. Several were
knowledgeably described by court writers who served the des-
potism that encouraged so many gifted artists. The age has been
assessed as a political failure, as ultraconservative and archaistic,
but in the arts it was richly, radically creative. Justinian's in-
ordinate ambition to glorify his reign was in this respect success-
ful, and it is just that we should associate the results with his
name. As a builder, he was a second Trajan, another Constantine.[25]

S. Vitale in Ravenna, the major Justinianic building in the West, was begun shortly before the completion of the imperial reconquest of Italy (plates 39 and 40). It is uncertain to what extent Justinian's agents, ecclesiastical and secular, were involved, but it is likely that the building from the first was conceived as a monument to Orthodoxy in the capital of the declining Arian kingdom of the Ostrogoths. The architect is unknown. but the building is a most exciting and challenging one.

The prismatic geometry and warm brick texture of the exterior envelop an exhilarating, expanding well of strongly verticalized interior space. The key to the design is in the ingenious reciprocal manner in which volumetric parts are interlocked. For example, the eastern apse and its flanking spaces are composed of cylinders, prisms, and blocks which pile up dramatically against the outer octagonal shell, carrying the eye continuously across a concatenated play of surfaces (plate 41). Each unit, delimited by the shadow lines of a sketchy terra-cotta cornice, can be read as an entity but is simultaneously joined and subordinated to the whole effect.

Striking as this unclassic treatment is, it is only the negative of the unbroken flux of spaces within (plate 42). Narrow, wedge-shaped piers, disposed at the points of an octagon and fenced by vaulted columnar exedrae, carry a high octagonal drum and a hemispherical dome reaching a hundred feet above the floor. Within the peripheral octagonal wall a two-story ring of aisles and galleries is fitted around this central void, broken only on the east by a deep longitudinal sanctuary radiant with mosaics of sacred events and the imperial court. The restlessness of the turning, polymorphic aisle and gallery spaces (plate 43) contrasts with the calm of the middle space, reaching above the surrounding forms to the brighter light of its clerestory. All vistas are complex, angled, incommensurable, a visual effect composed within an adroit structural system. The load-support relationship is obscured, for oblique thrusts are dispersed from the main piers through arches radiating over the galleries and aisles to secondary piers at the outer angles of the octagon. The whole is an organic perfection, a completed architecture.[26]

32

The principles which were so strikingly exhibited in S. Vitale were also given full play in Constantinople. Well-rehearsed vaulting techniques, an almost Roman mastery of the economy of building, and a legacy of Hellenistic design and geometry were put to use in the embellishment of the city. During his lifetime Justinian commissioned palaces, utilitarian and civic works, dozens of churches, and other structures.[27] They were built chiefly in the arcuate, domical style, richly colored, with an air of exotic, orientalized antiquity. Along the terraced land above the Sea of Marmora at the eastern limit of the city his predecessors had begun the Byzantine capitol (plate 44); to their buildings he added not only the present Hagia Sophia but major elements of the imperial palace and the neighboring churches of Hagia Eirene and SS. Sergius and Bacchus. Before his accession he presumably lived here by the shore in a subsidiary palace with galleries of vaulted bays behind a sober, arcuated sea façade (plate 44, F). To the north, beyond the Hippodrome and Forum, an enormous cistern was set into the ground, covered with hundreds of identical domical vaults ingeniously worked in brick. In this area, the heart of the Byzantine world, Justinianic style was fully stated.

At the center of the style lies the concept of the elevated central pavilion, or baldacchino form. The governing principles of sixth-century architecture, visual, empathic, and structural, are gathered and interlocked in this shape. It was used as a spatial unit, often reduplicated along single or multiple axes, and it was built in a wide range of sizes. More important, it expressed in its forms the domical image of heaven and the ancient canopied symbol of divine approval at the same time that it provided visual and functional space both through and between its vertical supports. In the major buildings harmonic variations on the same theme were set around the central space. This might be done in a radial symmetry, as at S. Vitale (plate 39), along a cross plan, as at Ephesus (plate 64), or within a noncongruent peripheral rectangle as at SS. Sergius and Bacchus and Hagia Sophia (plates 45 and 53). In each case a vertical frame was erected in which the members farthest from the center helped to support

33

the variety of curving vaults that were cast over the whole. By and large walls became adventitious, fitted where needed between the vertical members and continued up beneath the turning edges of the vaults. From the interior the major effect was of an assembly of shell-like ascents and returns between discrete verticals; subsidiary and nonstructural elements were also treated with embracing arched motives. With mosaic and polished marble surfaces washed by light from carefully scaled and positioned windows, or picked out by the flicker of hundreds of lamps dispersed through a hovering chromatic void, the Byzantine celebrant and worshiper were reverentially and gorgeously housed.

About the time of his accession, Justinian commissioned SS. Sergius and Bacchus, a design somewhat reminiscent of S. Vitale, but more closely related to Hagia Sophia in its rectangular encasement, axial linear column screens, and spreading Roman horizontality (plates 45–49).[28] It is typical of East Christian art that the building combines elements of such widely spread provenance as an extremely ancient masonry technique (vaults of slanted bricks), structural forms of Roman imperial derivation (the gored dome, the complex corner vaults), and carving of both late classical and specifically Byzantine style. But the creative sixth-century synthesis of these practices is only one aspect of an original design in which it is difficult not to see a study for Hagia Sophia. Irrespective of size, the similarities of the two buildings are far more telling than their differences, and it seems probable that they are the work of the same man. Whether or not this hypothesis is correct, the authorship of Hagia Sophia is not in doubt; for the first time since the age of Augustus we have the pleasure of knowing something about the life of an architect. For Hagia Sophia, the great church of Christ as the Holy Wisdom of God, was conceived by Anthemius, a natural scientist and geometer from Tralles in Asia Minor, and built by him in 532–537 in collaboration with Isidore of Miletus and Emperor Justinian.[29]

The commanding site of Hagia Sophia is magnificent; on three sides the land slopes gradually away to the shore. In

34

Christian times the church was flanked by the Patriarchate and a colonnaded forum to the south and by a spacious court to the west. Something of the vertical accent stated originally by an adjacent memorial column of Justinian and the tall gilded cross which crowned the central vault is powerfully restored by the Turkish minarets now standing at the four corners of the building. The exterior is massy, proportionately low for its length, and hedged in by a later accumulation of shoring masonry piles (plates 50 and 51). As at the Orthodox Baptistry the exterior was treated as only the necessary and ineradicable reverse of the interior experience which was the whole being and meaning of the building.

The walls and vaults are of brick set in very thick beds of mortar (plate 52), and the four major piers and the columns are of stone. The ribbed dome, slightly over a hundred feet in diameter, rests upon spherical pendentives supported by arches and piers on a square plan (plates 53 and 55). To the eastern and western arches are fitted half-domes which are in turn obliquely expanded by vaulted exedrae below them. Including the apse, an immense longitudinal floor space, two hundred and sixty feet in length, is opened up under a swelling, billowing canopy (plate 54). Flanking this space, and edging east and west toward its center line, are aisles and galleries of more human scale. They are divided by massive vaulted bridges passing from the central piers to the pendant tower buttresses on the north and south flanks of the central block from which the dome rises. The building is bilaterally but not radially symmetrical, for the north and south sides of the immense central pavilion are composed of linear column screens carrying tympanum walls fitted under the powerful arches above, and thus the distribution of thrusts is somewhat devious. The original shallow dome was replaced by the present higher, more secure construction late in Justinian's reign; even so, earthquakes caused failures of the less firmly buttressed western and eastern parts of the superstructure in the tenth and fourteenth centuries.

The interior achieves an unequaled effect of majestic weightlessness and profound harmony through a paradoxical, even

35

contradictory apposition of architectural phrasing. The whole is frame daround Anthemius' solution to the problem of combining a vertical symbolic center with a solemn processional axis. Buildings are by definition three-dimensional, but Hagia Sophia, it may be said, is intricately so (plate 56). The observer standing on the marble pavement of the nave is under the immediate influence of the horizontal plane of the longitudinal axis; a hundred and eighty-five feet above him soars the canopy of the dome. Between these two areas is a transitional space which belongs to both. The satellite half-domes of the middle level are axially connected, while their spreading surfaces and the adjacent pendentives are harmonic to the central vault above. The floated in-between world which these shapes suggest more than form is the key to the inseparable simultaneous operation of both axes.

Every aspect of the design works toward the desubstantiation of the physical reality of the building. The vault surfaces read as thin shells, and their intersections are tangential and largely unmolded (plate 57). Arched forms curve and overlap in continuing, fluid sequences. The pendentives die out into visually unsupported points. The masses of the great piers are removed from the nave space and are covered with colored marbles whose polished surfaces seem continuous with those of the marble columns, gold-ground mosaics, and wickered basketry of the capitals (plates 58 and 59). An energizing heliophany plays through the coronas of windows, adding a final visual and spiritual dimension (plate 60).

Hagia Sophia itself was never copied, either in scale or design, by Byzantine builders. But in Justinian's lifetime several other versions of the basic sixth-century scheme were built. In the Church of Hagia Eirene short barrel vaults form a cross about the central unit and a low dome covers an extended western nave (plate 61). The much-verticalized design of the church at Kasr-ibn-Wardan in northern Syria clearly was influenced by Hagia Sophia (plate 62), though no half-domes were used and the nave was compressed into little more than the space beneath the high dome. At Philippi in northern Greece a vaulted nave

36

was attached to a domed crossing in a rather perfunctory way (plate 63).[30]

In Constantinople Justinian replaced the fourth-century Church of the Holy Apostles with a very important and influential building composed of domed pavilion elements on a cross plan. The tomb-church of emperors, it was long ago destroyed, but literary descriptions and the foundations of a similar and contemporary church, S. John at Ephesus (plate 64), remain to give its general sense. The main axial space was formed of four domed bays, the penultimate over the crossing. Around the whole, including the domed arms of the transept, ran a continuous aisle. The influence of the Holy Apostles extended not only to Ephesus but to S. Marco in Venice (plate 93) and the domed Romanesque churches of Aquitaine (plate 97). In contrast, the mid-century basilica of S. Apollinare in Classe, near Ravenna, with its elegant external arcades and lucid composition, pointed toward the Lombard style (plate 65).[31]

The principal buildings of Justinian, unequivocally original, had a remarkably widespread influence not only upon the architecture of the Byzantine Empire but upon that of Slavic, Moslem, and Western lands as well. Behind this lustrous achievement lies the genius of Anthemius and the capacities of his colleagues and contemporaries; behind them, Justinian himself. Hagia Sophia, the mosaics of S. Vitale, and the preservation of Roman law can with some confidence be balanced against the darkness which the Emperor's military and territorial ambitions helped to draw across the exhausted Mediterranean world.

4 BYZANTINE ARCHITECTURE

Under most unpromising conditions the Byzantines fashioned a spiritual and material culture which came to be coveted by the surrounding world. From the sixth century until the beginning of the ninth they were engaged in external and internal struggles of the gravest nature. The tide of Islam swept back the southern and eastern frontiers. The government and the Church were locked in a fierce controversy about the propriety of image worship, and both narrowly missed extinction by chaotic extra-classical forces which the late antique world had barely excluded. The Empire survived because its comparatively orderly Roman frame was defended by heroic efforts and patched by compromise and adjustment. During the long struggle the medieval Byzantine state was formed; in the end high Byzantine culture emerged, a civilization in the ancient sense, dividing the shores of the Mediterranean with Islam.[32]

Byzantine institutions were seen as granted by God and presided over by the Emperor, and every facet of life reflected this doctrine. All centered in Constantinople, where an organized government painstakingly maintained that image of a great Christian prince, especially favored by God and armored with gold, of which the distant nations dreamed. There were certain indications that the image might be a reality. The government ruled far more by law than not, and the great city functioned much like its Hellenistic and Roman forebears. Fragments of the image, titles and symbols carefully measured for diplomatic effect, were condescendingly awarded to less-favored peoples, and from Constantinople the faith was propagated beyond the frontiers. The Church, theoretically at least, was held to be only one aspect of society, without authority independent of the state; the Patriarch did not take precedence over the Emperor. An ingenious suppleness of the government in foreign relations was paralleled ecclesiastically by the practice of granting newly converted peoples the privilege of using their own languages in the liturgy. Broadly speaking, the palace and the Church co-operated through the centuries, the ultimate legal authority resting in the palace. Power, patronage, and status were the gift of the sacred Emperor, whose charism was sustained by a ceremonial and an architecture intentionally mirroring the courts of heaven.

After Justinian's death the construction of public churches nearly ceased, and for three centuries the palace was the only really important building site (plate 66). An intricacy of varied structures spread gradually from the original palace of Constantine by the Hippodrome. Only a few foundations (plate 44) and textual references remain, together with a tenth-century record of the elaborate court ceremonies; paper reconstructions of the palace are extremely conjectural.[33] Yet two buildings, perhaps the most important ones, emerge more clearly than the rest. One, the Chrysotriclinos, was a late sixth-century audience hall rich with golden mosaics. Octagonal in plan and lit by sixteen dome windows, its apse housed the throne; throughout, the building published the secular dogma of the court. The other was the Church of Our Lady of the Pharos, commissioned in about 860 by Emperor Michael III and surely a seminal design of the first rank. The Nea Ecclesia, or New Church, built in the palace grounds by Emperor Basil I about 880, was probably of similar design (plate 67; foundations possibly those marked C on plate 44).

In a homily delivered in 864 the Patriarch Photius described the decoration of the Pharos church, the chapel of the emperors adjoining the Chrysotriclinos. From this description the general form emerges. A dome and pendentive pavilion unit stood at the center and three apses were grouped at the east end. There are churches of slightly later date extant in Constantinople that were almost certainly derived directly from the Pharos church and the Nea. From these it is reasonable to infer a cross-in-square plan in the manner of Musmiyeh and Gerasa (plates 18 and 23), barrel-vaulted cross arms, and vaulted elements over the residual corner areas. The central dome, of segmental or ribbed construction, did not spring directly from a pendentive ring but was elevated upon a cylinder or drum, adding a measure of verticality lacking in the neighboring sixth-century churches. Probably the diagonally placed corner vaults were elevated, though to a less degree, in a similar fashion. The reciprocities between the symbolic and processional spaces and balanced structural dispositions were nicely calculated. The shapes of the Pharos church, culminating in the central vault, were fittingly prepared for their sheath of hierarchically arranged mosaics: the Pantocrator (Christ as the Judge of All) in the central dome, with angels and evangelists in the drum and pendentives, the Virgin in the quarter-sphere vault of the apse, and sacred scenes, saints, and hierarchs below. Because of its magnificently appropriate form and august origins, the Pharos type became the chief inspiration for Orthodox church architecture.[34]

The city itself clearly proclaimed its classical ancestry.[35] Public squares or fora, islands of communal space announced by triumphal arches, were dispersed through the packed wards. Major axes of the city, colonnaded or arcaded thoroughfares lined with shops, were fixed by towering memorial columns. There were orphanages, hospitals, hostelries, restaurants, taverns, police stations, magistrates' courts, and street-lighting and fire brigades—all directly descended from classical models. A central milestone and a senate house recalled the antique originals in Italy, and the fora and principal baths were encrusted with sculpture from Greece and Rome. The four magnificent horses now in Venice were displayed high above the Hippodrome track, and the monument to the victors of Plataea, once dedicated at Delphi, stood nearby. Architecture for such a city would naturally be conceived in sympathy with classical ideals and perceptions, and would be influenced by classical qualities of design.

Indeed, the splendid churches erected in Constantinople during the two or three centuries after the building of the Pharos church were based, ultimately, upon classical principles of suitable and precise harmony of parts and the shaping of architecture to relate man to his aspirations. Several of these churches still exist, though crippled by time and altered by later Turkish reconstructions; from them the principles of the magnificent middle Byzantine style can be inferred.[36] In these buildings the general scheme of the Pharos church was freely interpreted on a smaller scale (plate 68). Elevated drums, creating more vertical silhouettes, became canonical, though the satellite corner vaults were sometimes held to gallery roof level (plate 69). Elegant exteriors were fashioned either of brick, which was sometimes set in colored mortar, or of alternating bands of brick and stone. Tall, narrow niches ate into these surfaces, lessening the mass of the walls and emphasizing the rising lines of the design. The eaves lines were accented by rich articulations in molded terracotta forms and by bricks set diagonally in a fashion reminiscent of S. Vitale (plates 69–71).

The tenth-century church which may be that of the Myrelaion monastery is an example both of the style generally and of the high degree of individuality usually found within it (plate 70). Here the four central supports are piers, and the arms of

42

the cross and the low residual chambers are groin-vaulted. Both the drum and the dome are formed on the interior of sixteen concave panels, which in the zone of the drum are alternately pierced by windows and backed by engaged buttresses of triangular section. Interest in exterior design reappears. The building is strengthened by engaged buttresses of curving sections which, though they emphasize the verticality of the composition, are tied by a thin horizontal string course which lightly pulls the inflected surfaces together. The interior shapes of the building are as apparent from the outside as before, but they are now made the mechanism from which an exterior architecture is developed.[37]

As in so much Byzantine art, the effect of these churches was one of sumptuous elegance brilliantly and inextricably united with symbolic forms. Within this unity the flowing spaces, encased in an envelope of color, were functionally disposed for liturgical requirements. A deep, vaulted sanctuary and apse, communicating laterally with flanking side-chambers, housed the altar. A screen of painted icons stood athwart the main axis just beyond the eastern columns. Narthexes, and perhaps side porches, effected spatial and visual transition between the outer world and the jewel-like interiors. Incense, chant, ecclesiastical vestments, and ancient rites were combined with architecture and mosaic to evoke for the spirit and the senses that vision of another world around which Byzantine life revolved.

The Crusades, the Latin occupation of Constantinople, and the subsequent acquisition of the provinces by encroaching powers reduced the resources but not the artistic capacities of the Byzantines. A part of the so-called Palace of Constantine Porphyrogenitus, probably of the thirteenth century, marks the continuity between the nave arcades of Hagia Sophia and medieval Venetian façades with broad ground-story openings rhythmically echoed by banded reveals of reduced scale above (plate 72; cf. plate 80). Nearby, in the northernmost quarter of the city, the early fourteenth-century cycle of mosaics in the Church of the Chora rank among the finest of all medieval works of art. Even they are equaled, perhaps surpassed, by the moving beauty of contemporary wall paintings in a side chapel of the same church.[38] Upon varied curved surfaces set above a basilican space, the images of the Last Judgment and the Virgin surrounded by angels preside over figures of hierarchs and saints below. In the apse vault a luminous, majestic figure of Christ raises Adam and Eve in the presence of the Righteous, a painting of incomparable grandeur and power (plate 73). A few generations later the city was taken by the Ottoman Turks, but over the centuries the architecture and art of Constantinople had radiated to the provinces and beyond.

The churches of Armenia, dating from the seventh century onward, belong to the same broad architectural current as post-Justinianic buildings in Constantinople, though the relationships between the two groups are obscure.[39] Concepts from Parthia and Syria are apparent in polyfoil plans and intricate many-sided volumes, as at S. Hrip'simé, an early seventh-century building (plate 74). These, however, are ancillary to the aspects of Armenian architecture that gave it an individuality. The carefully fitted ashlar masonry of the casing walls (enclosing rubble concrete fillings) defines a crystalline sharpness of form not found to the west or south. These forms are tall rather than broad, built of flat surfaces bounding crisp tent shapes and gables (plate 75). Vertical surfaces are often deeply grooved by tall, narrow niches, and at the Church of the Cross at Aght'amar of the early ninth century the exterior is decorated by projecting bands and groups of relief celebrating Armenian life and history as well as Old and New Testament scenes (plate 76). Little if anything of the curving interior surfaces, fashioned by an almost High Gothic mastery of the stereometry of stonecutting, is conveyed to the exterior shapes. In their dense, almost jagged forms, the Armenian churches reflect the masses and profiles of the majestic mountain ranges against which they are set.

Farther to the southeast and south, the churches of Mesopotamia, Persia, Egypt, Nubia, and Ethiopia were to some extent related to the architecture of Constantinople.[40] This relationship was both direct and collateral, stemming partly from a common root in early Christian architecture. Local building

44

traditions, particular rites, building methods and materials intervened to form quasi-Byzantine styles.

Much more closely related to the Constantinople buildings are the numerous medieval churches of the Byzantine province of Greece, though here, too, there are important local permutations. With the exception of the church of the Convent of the Assumption at Daphni (plates 77 and 78) and that of S. Luke of Stiris (plate 79), both of the eleventh century, they are as little known as their contemporaries in the capital. At Daphni and Stiris the preservation of the mosaics is such that the buildings can give a sense of what the interrelationship of architecture and decoration would have been like in the Pharos church and its progeny. The mosaic figures are made of small splintery cubes of richly colored glass, and are set against featureless fields of transparent cubes enclosing thin sheets of gold. Projected from webs of light gathered in their golden backgrounds, the elevated sacred effigies appear to inhabit the airy volumes under the vaults. They are weightless icons, almost afloat in spaces defined by surfaces that seem more suspended than supported. Below, lesser personages are ranged upon the walls and piers. The interior of the Byzantine church, by obliterating the distinction between architecture and decoration, became a magical image of the Christian cosmos.[41]

Neither S. Luke nor Daphni uses the four-column system; their drums and domes are placed above square plans by means of half-cone shapes which bridge the corners of the squares to form octagons, a common solution in southern Greece. The exteriors do not convey the sense of height given by the interiors. Walls are usually of stone and brick combined; the window openings are outlined in brick and divided into two or three sections by mullion columns, forming diminutive arcades, a distinguishing feature of Byzantine architecture. The whole may be contained in rather Constantinopolitan forms, as at Daphni, or enclosed within a high-shouldered block as in a church at Arta (plate 80), of unusual interior engineering. Throughout Greece later versions of the general scheme exist, sometimes defined in an abstract, undecorated geometry of simplicity (plate 81).

45

The churches of Salonica are even more closely allied with Constantinople than those of southern and central Greece.[42] Hagia Sophia, probably dating from the early eighth century and a rare example of a church built during the famous iconoclastic controversy owes an obvious debt to its great namesake while retaining a heavy Roman feeling (cf. plate 27). The later Salonica churches are, however, fairly directly derived from the Pharos-Nea group. Sometimes with ambulatories passing around the whole cross-in-square four-column system, they are intimately scaled parish versions of the imperial foundations (plate 82). Their forms of warmly colored brick are stitched together by niches, stilted arches, and belt and saw-tooth cornices. They were executed *con brio* for congregations of less presumption than those of the capital. The imposing forms of Constantinople gave way to a certain intimacy, due to diminished size; the corner drums and domes of the Salonica churches can shelter only a few persons. At the same time verticality increased proportionately as the drums, capped by their exuberant cornices, were pulled farther up.

On the peninsula of Mount Athos, reserved for monasteries, another variant of the Byzantine church appeared. There the four-column system was often embraced on three sides by semicircular apses in order properly to house the monks' particular liturgical usages (plate 83). The peninsula is scattered with improvisations upon the familiar forms (plate 84), which are echoed also at Mistra in the Peloponnesus, the home of the last imperial dynasty and, like Athos, a museum of late Byzantine architecture on an isolated, mountainous site (plate 85).[43]

Beyond the western and northern frontiers the Byzantine style merged in varying degrees with local inspiration. In old Serbia the Salonican designs, passed up the Vardar valley in the twelfth and thirteenth centuries, helped to shape important Balkan schools. Generally speaking, these buildings are tight, constricted versions of the Byzantine scheme, bundles of vertical shafts of space terminating in distant, luminous capsules (plates 86 and 87). Further north, the standard central element was sometimes enclosed in medieval north Italian forms (plate 88).[44]

Similarly, early Russian monumental church architecture was partly of Byzantine inspiration.[45] The Russians, converted by Byzantium to Christianity at the end of the tenth century, made direct use of the Byzantine style during the eleventh century, as at S. Sophia in Kiev (plates 89 and 90), since much altered and elaborated. In the next century, Russian architecture drew upon Byzantine sources as well as upon Caucasian and far northern styles (plates 91 and 92). The operatic, vividly colored style of onion domes above proliferating roof lines appeared subsequently; in it, a thread of Byzantine continuity can still be seen.

In Italy Byzantine architecture was influential for several centuries in Venice, the lands of the Exarchate centering on Ravenna and the far south. In time its influence waned, like the *maniera greca* of painting, leaving behind S. Marco, a diminutive chapel in S. Prassede in Rome, a number of modest churches in Apulia and Calabria, and the splendid mosaic churches of the Normans in northern Sicily. S. Marco in Venice, though caparisoned with additions of later centuries, is a Byzantine design of the eleventh century (plates 93 and 94). From a cross plan with arms of equal length, five domed-pavilion units rise. They form under their tautly stretched surfaces two lofty intersecting halls richly inlaid with mosaics of several periods (plate 95); this timeless Byzantine world contrasts sharply with the Gothic combs and pneumatic superstructure of the exterior (plate 96).[46] The basic scheme appears again at S. Front in Périgueux, largely of the twelfth century, but translated into a Romanesque vocabulary (plate 97). Without mosaics or marbles, proudly showing its medieval French fabric, S. Front is at the far edge of Byzantine influence.[47]

The Byzantine occupation of the southernmost parts of Italy for five centuries and the subsequent Norman use of Byzantine builders and artists explain the presence there of so many familiar forms. Humble variants upon eastern designs appear frequently in the impoverished lands south of Naples, interspersed with an occasional sensitive and individualized design such as that of the church at Stilo in Calabria (plate 98).[48] There the five-dome scheme is rendered in clear, simple forms. The vaults are capped

47

by low, spreading saucer-roofs, the drums enlivened with diamond patterns and saw-tooth cinctures. In and near Palermo, a Byzantine architectural frontier like southwestern France, there is a rich assembly of Byzantine art.[49] In addition to the major churches of Monreale, Cefalu, and Palermo proper (the Palatine Chapel of the Normans; La Martorana), there are exotic structures such as S. John of the Hermits (plate 99), where African, Byzantine, and other worlds mix. At Stilo the bright earth colors are enriched by contrast with the blue-gray rock of the naked mountains; at S. John rose-orange domes are set against the sky.

Most of these buildings so distant from Constantinople were built during the political decline of the Empire. By the fifteenth century it had shrunk to little more than the capital and parts of Greece, and could not resist the energy and cannon of the Turks, who succeeded where Goths, Germans, Huns, Bulgars, Arabs, and Russians had failed. A final mass was celebrated in Hagia Sophia on the night of May 28, 1453; the next day by the great walls the last Roman Emperor, Constantine XI, died defending his city.[50]

The story has no end. The Orthodox Church continues the patterns begun so long ago. Early Christian and Byzantine designs have been revived in recent times (plate 100), though not to the extent that Western medieval architecture has been reproduced. Both basilican and centralized church buildings deeply conditioned Moslem architecture, particularly Ottoman masterpieces by Sinan and others.[51] When Renaissance architects sought to learn from buildings of ancient Rome, they went to the same sources that had helped to shape medieval Christian buildings, and they created a style whose consanguinity with early Christian and Byzantine architecture has yet to be properly explored. In the recurrent rhythms of Mediterranean life, that architecture is a force alive.

1. Map of sites mentioned in the text.

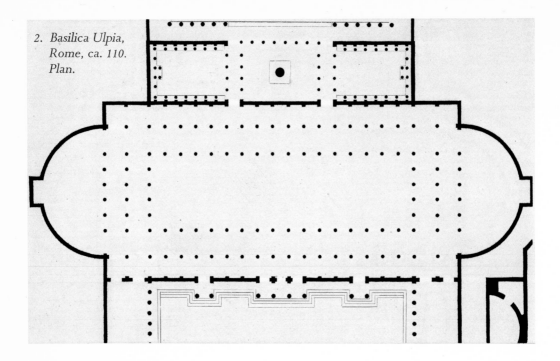

2. *Basilica Ulpia,*
   Rome, ca. 110.
   Plan.

3. *Basilica in the Imperial Palace,*
   Rome, ca. 85. Plan and section.

4. *Underground Basilica near the Porta*
   Maggiore, Rome, mid-first century. Plan.

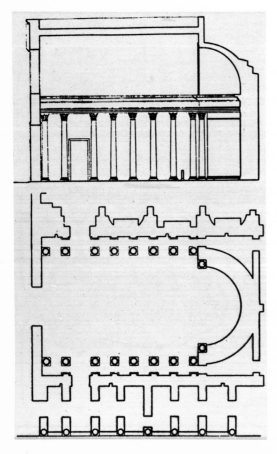

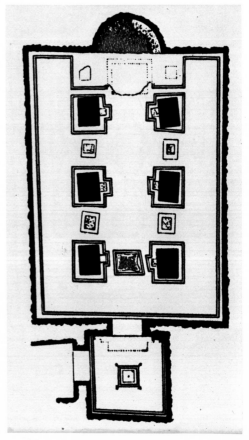

5. S. Paul's Outside the Walls, Rome, late fourth century. Engraving of interior.

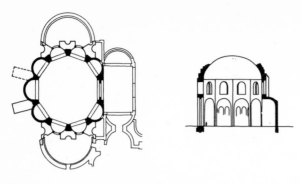

6. *Temple of Minerva Medica, Rome, ca. 320. Plan and section.*

7. *Temple of Minerva Medica. Model.*

8. *An Early Christian chancel, restored (SS. Peter and Paul, Gerasa).*

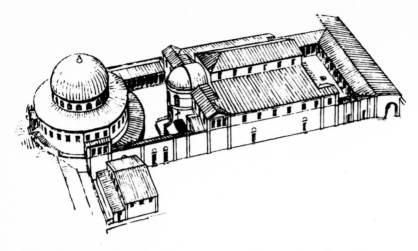

9. *Holy Sepulchre, Jerusalem, begun ca. 326. Restoration of exterior.*

10. *Holy Sepulchre, Rotunda of the Anastasis. Restoration as of ca. 348.*

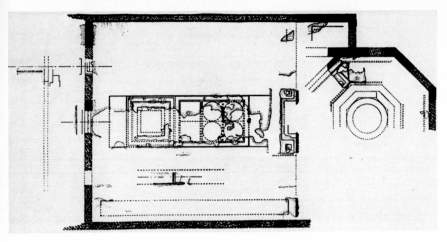

11. Church of the Nativity, Bethlehem, begun ca. 326. Plan of original building.

12. Old S. Peter's, Rome, ca. 333. Plan.

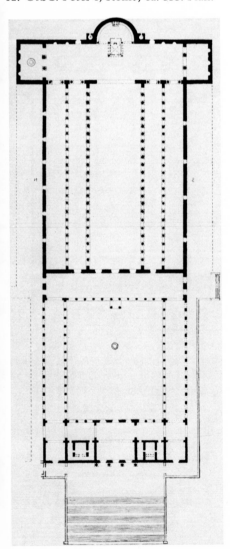

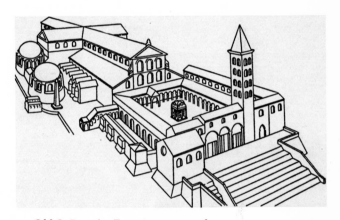

13. Old S. Peter's. Exterior, restored.

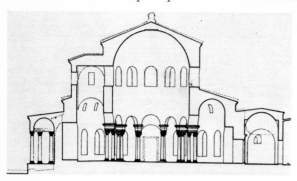

14. S. Costanza, Rome, perhaps 340. Plan and section.

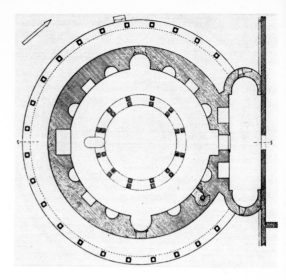

15. S. Costanza. Exterior.

16. *S. Costanza. Interior.*

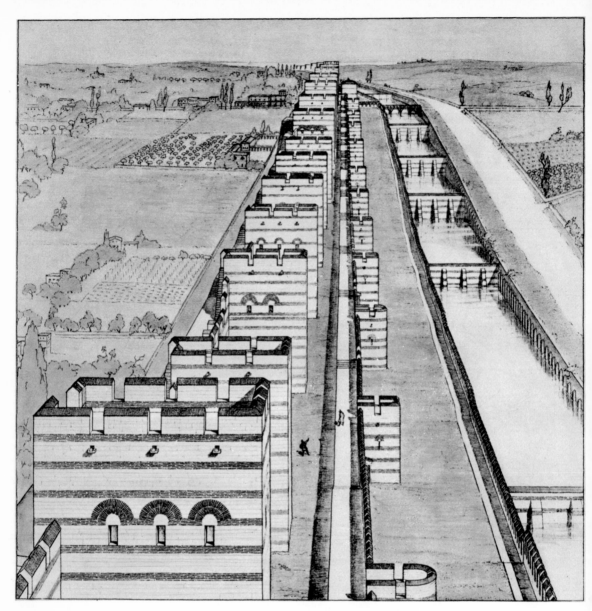

17. Land walls, Constantinople, first half of the fifth century. Restored.

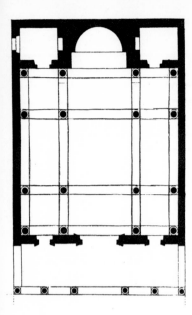

18. Praetorium-Church,
    Musmiyeh, ca. 160 and
    altered ca. 400. Plan.

19. Praetorium-Church. Interior.

20. Church of S. Simeon, near Aleppo, ca. 450–80. Plan.

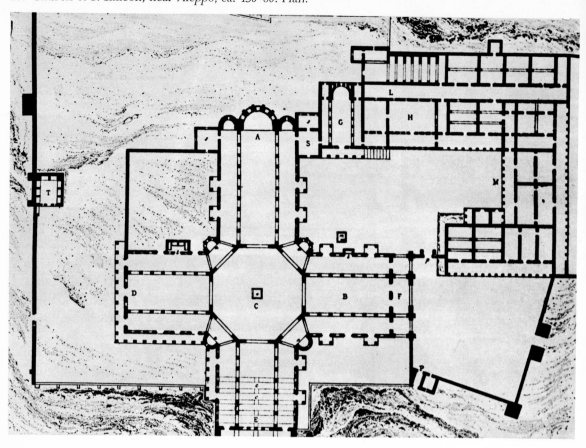

21. Church of S. Simeon. Restoration of the exterior.

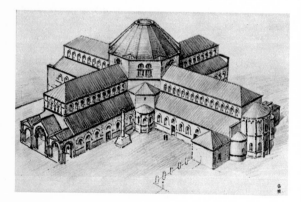

22. Church of S. Simeon. Detail of an apse.

23. *Church of the Prophets, Apostles and Martyrs, Gerasa, 464. Plan.*

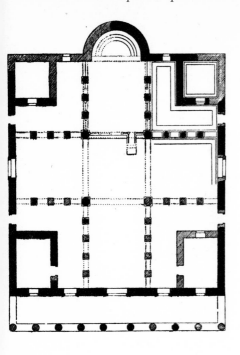

24. *Cathedral, Bosra, 513. Plan and section.*

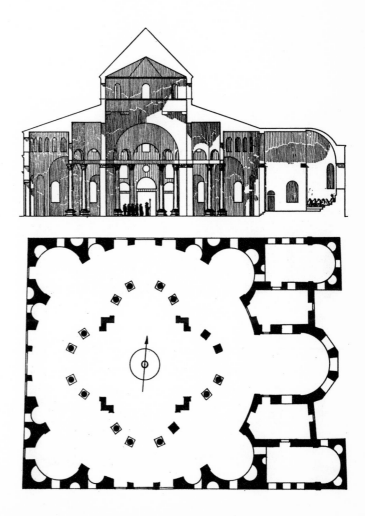

25. *Basilica at Der Turmanin, probably sixth century. Exterior, restored.*

26. *Alahan Kilise in Cilicia, late fifth or early sixth century. Plan.*

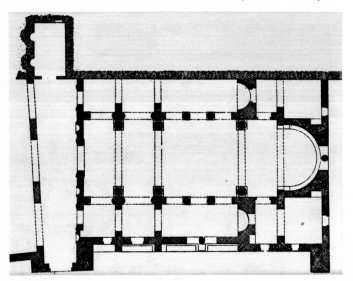

27. S. George, Salonica, ca. 310, altered in the fifth century. Interior view.

29. S. John of the Studion, Constantinople, late fifth century. Plan.

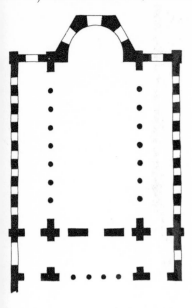

30. S. John of the Studion. Detail of porch.

31. S. Sabina, Rome, 425–32. Exterior.

32. S. Sabina. Interior

33. *S. Apollinare Nuovo, Ravenna, ca. 500. Interior.*

34. *Mausoleum of Galla Placidia, Ravenna, middle of the fifth century. Exterior.*

35. *Orthodox Baptistry, Ravenna, early, and then middle, fifth century. Interior.*

36. *Orthodox Baptistry. Plan.*

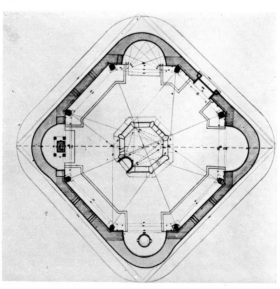

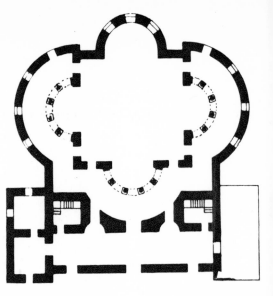

38. *Church or Audience Hall in Hadrian's Stoa, Athens, early fifth century. Plan.*

39. *S. Vitale, Ravenna, ca. 530–48. Plan.*

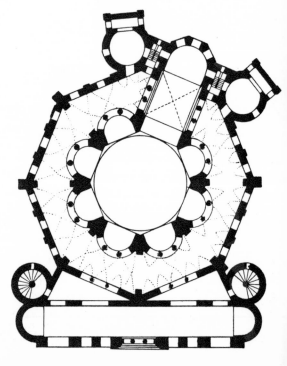

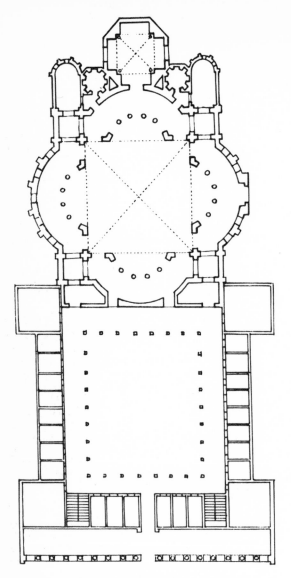

37. *S. Lorenzo Maggiore, Milan, ca. 460. Plan.*

41. S. Vitale. Exterior view of east end.

42. S. Vitale. Interior looking east.

43. *S. Vitale. Interior detail of aisle.*

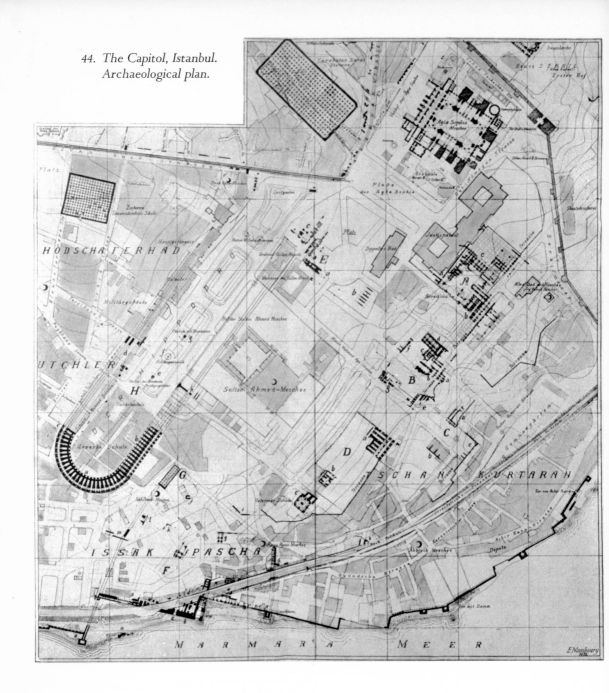

44. The Capitol, Istanbul.
Archaeological plan.

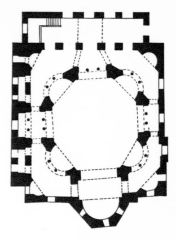

45. *SS. Sergius and Bacchus, Istanbul, ca. 527. Plan.*

46. *SS. Sergius and Bacchus. Exterior looking west.*

47. *SS. Sergius and Bacchus. Longitudinal section.*

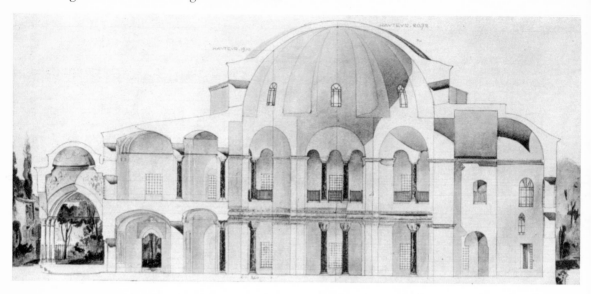

48. *SS. Sergius and Bacchus. Interior.*

50. *Hagia Sophia, Istanbul, 532–37 and 558–63. Exterior from southeast.*

51. *Hagia Sophia. Air view.*

52. *Hagia Sophia. Detail of masonry.*

53. *Hagia Sophia. Plan.*

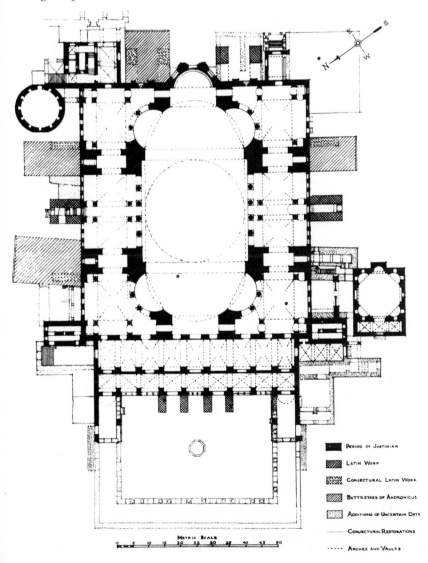

PERIOD OF JUSTINIAN

LATIN WORK

CONJECTURAL LATIN WORK

BUTTRESSES OF ANDRONICUS

ADDITIONS OF UNCERTAIN DATE

CONJECTURAL RESTORATIONS

ARCHES AND VAULTS

METRIC SCALE
0 5 10 15 20 25 30 35 40 45 50

54. Hagia Sophia. Painting of interior.

55. Hagia Sophia. Analytical half-section.

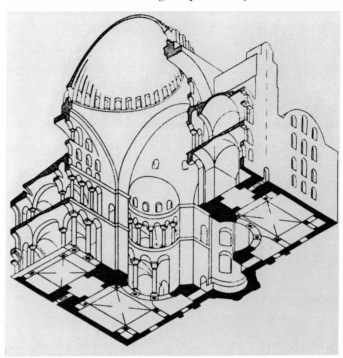

56. Hagia Sophia. Model showing the nave space as a solid.

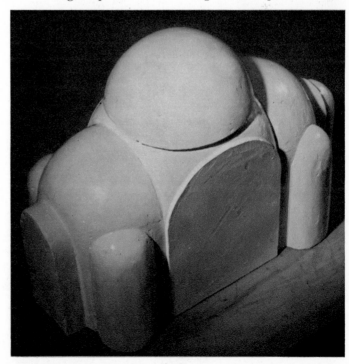

57. *Hagia Sophia. Interior, view of north and northwest superstructure.*

58. *Hagia Sophia. Marble revetment.*

59. *Hagia Sophia. Capitals and mosaic sheathing.*

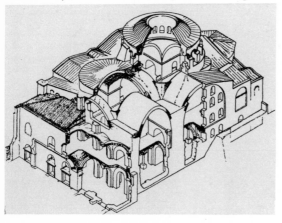

61. Hagia Eirene, Istanbul, middle of the sixth century, later altered. Analytical drawing.

62. Church at Kasr-ibn-Wardan, 564. Section.

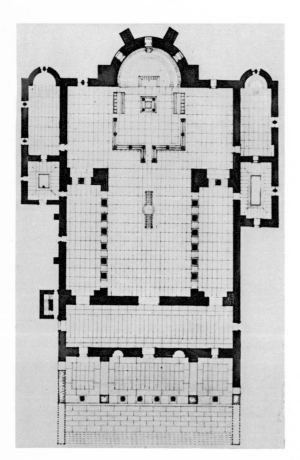

63. Basilica " B," Philippi, ca. 560. Plan.

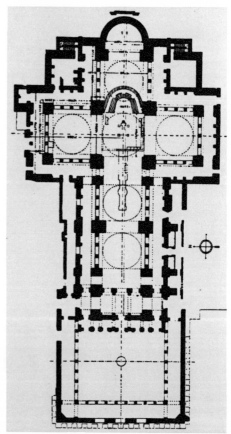

64. S. John, Ephesus, middle of the sixth century. Plan.

65. S. Apollinare in Classe, near Ravenna, 549. Air view.

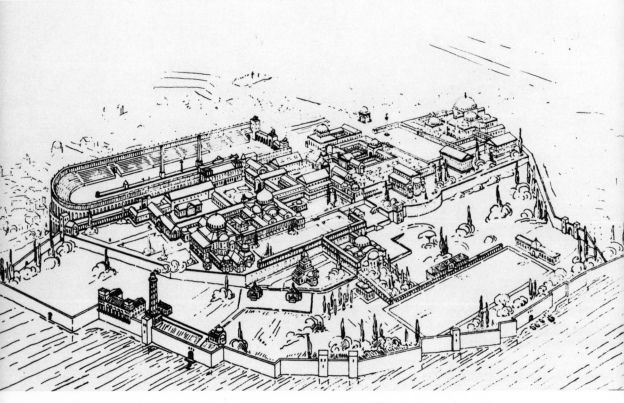

66. *The Great Palace of the Byzantine Emperors, Istanbul, fourth through tenth centuries. Conjectural perspective restoration, as of ca. 950.*

67. Nea Ecclesia, Istanbul, 880. Restored plan.

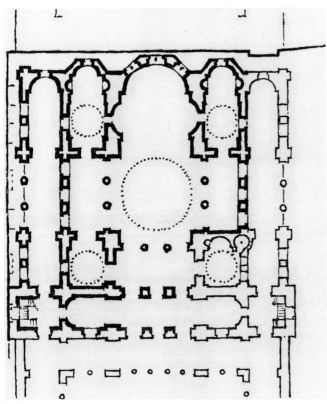

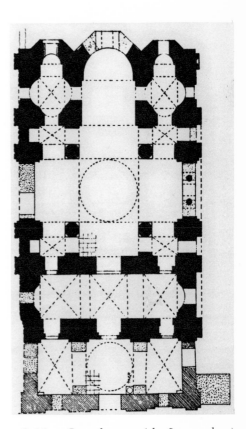

*68. S. Mary Panachrantos (the Immaculate),
Istanbul, perhaps 904. Plan.*

69. *S. Theodosia, Istanbul, perhaps 1000. Exterior.*

70. *Church of the Myrelaion Monastery, Istanbul, probably middle of the tenth century. Exterior.*

71. *S. Mary Pammakaristos (the All-Blessed), Istanbul, thirthteenth century. Exterior.*

72. *"Palace of Constantine Porphyrogenitus", Istanbul, probably thirteenth century. Exterior of southern façade.*

73. *Mural paintings in the side chapel of the Church of the Chora, Istanbul, ca. 1310–20.*

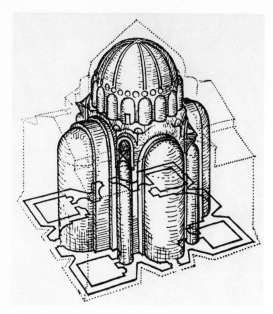

74. *S. Hrip'simé, Vagharshapat, 618. Analytical drawing.*

75. *Church at Aght'amar, 915–21. Exterior.*

76. *Church at Aght'amar. Exterior detail.*

77. Convent Church, Daphni, late eleventh century. Mosaics.

78. Convent Church. Exterior.

79. Churches of S. Luke and the Virgin, Stiris, eleventh century. Exterior from the east.

82. Church of the Holy Apostles, Salonica, 1312–15. Exterior.

83. Church of Docheiariou, Athos, probably thirteenth century. Plan.

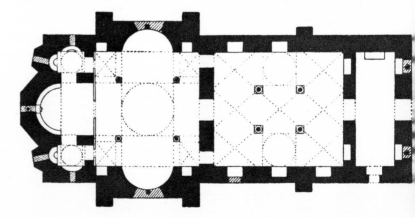

84. *A Church at the Great Lavra, Athos, probably largely sixteenth century. Exterior from above.*

85. S. Mary Pantanassa (Queen of All), Mistra, 1428. Exterior.

86. *Monastery Church at Gracanica, 1321. Exterior.*

87. *Monastery Church. Plan.*

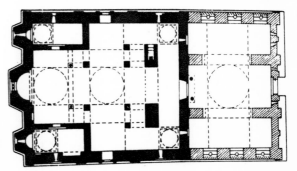

88. Church of the Virgin, Monastery of Studenica, 1183–91. Exterior.

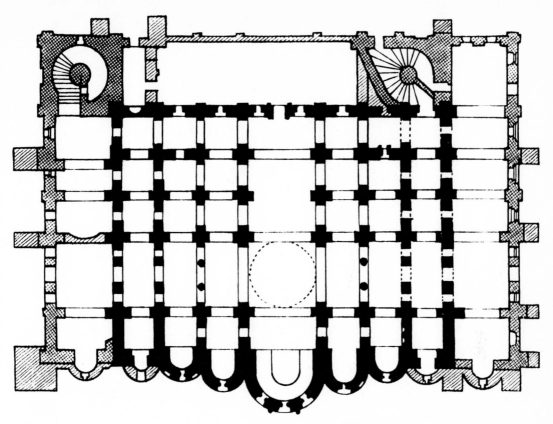

89. S. Sophia, Kiev, begun 1037. Plan.

90. S. Sophia. Restored exterior view.

91. *Church of the Intercession of the Virgin, on the River Nerl, near Vladimir, 1166. Exterior.*

92. *Cathedral of the Assumption, Vladimir, 1189. Exterior.*

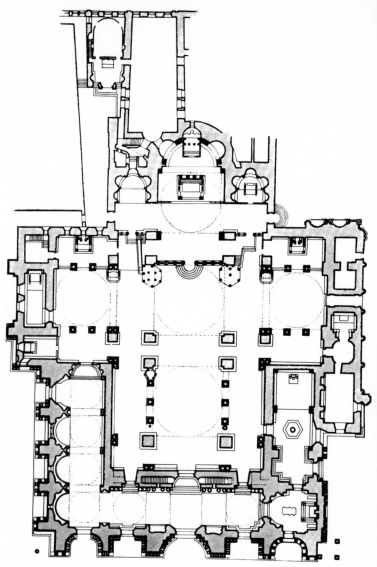

93. S. Marco, Venice, ca. 1063–94, many later alternations. Plan.

94. S. Marco. Exterior detail.

96. S. Marco. Exterior looking east.

97. S. Front, Périgueux, 1047 and following. Interior.

98. *La Cattolica, Stilo, probably eleventh century. Exterior from above.*

99. S. John of the Hermits, Palermo, 1132–48. Exterior.

100. S. Esprit, Paris, 1930–35. Exterior of superstructure.

NOTES

1. Lactantius, *De mortibus persecutorum*, xlviii. There is another version in Eusebius' *Ecclesiastical History*, X, v. This is all there is of the "Edict of Milan."

2. The earliest Christians assembled in houses that sometimes had been altered internally for liturgical use. A house-church of about 240 was found at Dura-Europos on the Euphrates; M. Rostovtzeff, *Dura-Europos and its Art*, Oxford, 1938, pp. 130 ff.

3. See G. Bandmann, *Mittelalterliche Architektur als Bedeutungsträger*, Berlin, 1952, pp. 45 ff. These relationships are also discussed by J. B. Ward Perkins, in "Constantine and the Origins of the Christian Basilica," *Papers of the British School in Rome*, XXII, 1954, pp. 69 ff., and in "The Italian

Element in Late Roman and Early Medieval Architecture," *Proceedings of the British Academy,* XXXIII, 1947, pp. 163 ff.

4. See F. E. Brown, *Roman Architecture,* New York, 1961.

5. This of necessity oversimplifies; the complexities can be seen in L. Crema, *L'architettura romana,* Turin, 1959, the most thorough handbook.

6. The structure of this kind of building is discussed by G. Giovannoni, in C. Bailey, ed., *The Legacy of Rome,* Oxford, 1923, pp. 429 ff.

7. Timber roofs were more common over the tower or pavilion elements than the vaults that are frequently shown in restorations; see G. Forsyth, "Architectural Notes on a Trip through Cilicia," *Dumbarton Oaks Papers,* XI, 1957, pp. 223 ff.

8. The existence of such an office is a reasonable inference from textual and other evidence; see R. MacMullen, "Roman Imperial Building in the Provinces," *Harvard Studies in Classical Philology,* 64, 1959, pp. 207 ff.

9. J. B. Bury, *History of the Later Roman Empire,* Vol. I, London, 1931, Chap. 1 and 2; for the effect of this upon the arts, see A. Grabar, *L'empereur dans l'art byzantin,* Paris, 1936.

10. N. H. Baynes, "Constantine the Great and the Christian Church," *Proceedings of the British Academy,* XV, 1929.

11. J. R. Palanque and others, *The Church in the Christian Roman Empire,* trans. by E. C. Messenger, Vol. I, London, 1949, Part I, Chap. 1, and Part II, in addition to N. H. Baynes, *op. cit.*

12. K. J. Conant, "The Original Buildings at the Holy Sepulchre in Jerusalem, "*Speculum,* XXXI, 1956, pp. 1 ff.; J. W. Crowfoot, *Early Churches in Palestine,* London, 1941, Chap. 1 and 2.

13. Information about the basilica comes in part from a letter from Constantine to a Bishop of Jerusalem; L. H. Vincent and F. M. Abel, *Jerusalem,* II, Paris, 1914, p. 207. The site is described by Eusebius in his *Vita Constantini,* iii.

14. In the Campanian atrium house and in all known imperial palaces from those of the Flavians (A. D. 69–96) onward.

15. Crowfoot, *op. cit.*, pp. 22 ff. The church was rebuilt by Justinian.
16. J. B. Ward Perkins, *op. cit.*
17. Described by G. T. Rivoira, *Roman Architecture*, trans. by G. M. Rushforth, London, 1925, pp. 238 ff. See also K. Lehmann, "The Dome of Heaven," *Art Bulletin*, XXVII, 1945.
18. For Constantinople, G. Downey, *Constantinople in the Age of Justinian*, Norman, Okla., 1960; and R. Janin, *Constantinople byzantin*, Paris, 1950. For the nature of Byzantine civilization, N. H. Baynes and H. Moss, *Byzantium*, Oxford, 1948.
19. For Syrian buildings, see H. C. Butler, *Ancient Architecture in Syria*, 2 vols., Leyden, 1907–1920, and *Early Churches in Syria*, Princeton, 1929. Musmiyeh is best treated by E. Weigand, "Das sogenannte Praetorium von Phaena-Mismije," *Würzburger Studien*, XIII, 1938, pp. 71 ff. For the Gerasa church, see C. Kraeling, ed., *Gerasa*, New Haven, 1938, pp. 256 ff.
20. M. Golding, "The Cathedral at Bosra," *Archaeology*, I, 1948, pp. 150 ff. For possible Syrian-Romanesque relationships, H. Schaeffer, "The Origin of the Two-Tower Façade in Romanesque Architecture," *Art Bulletin*, XXVII, 1945, pp. 98 ff.
21. For Alahan Kilise, see Forsyth, *op. cit.* Building methods and materials are discussed by J. B. Ward Perkins in D. Talbot Rice, ed., *The Great Palace of the Byzantine Emperors, Second Report*, Edinburgh, 1958, Chap. 3.
22. There are structures of almost purely Italian conception and construction in Asia Minor dating from the second and third centuries, at Ephesus, Miletus, Pergamum, Nicaea, and many other places.
23. The question of the relative weight that should be given to Eastern and Italian influences upon the design of these buildings has all but precluded the study of the monuments themselves. For an antidote, see Perkins, *Papers . . .*, *loc. cit.*
24. The Ravenna buildings have not been adequately published.

Much of the existing literature is covered by O. G. von Simson, *Sacred Fortress*, Chicago, 1948, and the buildings and their mosaics and carvings are illustrated in F. W. Deichmann, *Frühchristliche Bauten und Mosaiken von Ravenna*, Baden-Baden, 1958. For the Milan building, A. Calderini and others, *La basilica di S. Lorenzo Maggiore in Milano*, Milan, 1951; for the Athens building, M. A. Sisson, "The Stoa of Hadrian at Athens," *Papers of the British School at Rome*, XI, 1929, pp. 66 ff. For symbolism and meaning of the decoration of central vaults, K. Lehmann, *op. cit.*

25. The extensive works of the contemporary historian Procopius have been published, with a translation, in the Loeb Classical Library series. For modern views of the age, see J. B. Bury, *op. cit.*, II, or P. Ure, *Justinian and His Age*, Pelican Books, 1951.

26. There is no substantial work on San Vitale. It is described by G. T. Rivoira, *Lombardic Architecture*, trans. by G. M. Rushforth, Vol. I, Oxford, 1933, pp. 62 ff., and discussed in W. R. von Zaloziecky, "Ein stilgeschichtlicher Vergleich der Sergius Bacchus Kirche in Konstantinopel und S. Vitale in Ravenna," *Studi bizantini e neoellenici*, VI, 1940.

27. See G. Downey, "Justinian as Builder," *Art Bulletin*, XXXII, 1950, pp. 262 ff., and his *Constantinople, op. cit.*

28. J. Ebersolt, *Les églises de Constantinople*, Paris, 1913, pp. 21 ff. and plates; A. E. Henderson, "SS. Sergius and Bacchus, Constantinople," *The Builder*, XC, 1906, pp. 4 ff.; W. R. von Zaloziecky, *op. cit.*, pp. 452 ff.

29. On Anthemius, see G. L. Huxley, *Anthemius of Tralles, A Study in Later Greek Geometry*, Cambridge, Mass., 1959, and G. Downey, "Byzantine Architects, Their Training and Methods," *Byzantion*, XVIII, 1946–1948, pp. 99 ff. For Hagia Sophia, see E. H. Swift, *Hagia Sophia*, New York, 1940; W. R. Zaloziecky, *Die Sophienkirche in Konstantinopel*, Rome, 1936; W. R. Emerson and R. L. Van Nice, "Hagia Sophia, Istanbul," *American Journal of Archaeology*, XLVII, 1943, pp. 402 ff., "Hagia Sophia: The Collapse of the First Dome," *Archaeology*, IV, 1951, pp. 94 ff., "Hagia Sophia:

The Construction of the Second Dome and Its Later Repairs," *Archaeology*, IV, 1951, pp. 162 ff.; W. L. MacDonald, "Design and Technology in Hagia Sophia," *Perspecta*, IV, 1957, pp. 20 ff. Some of the major aspects of Hellenistic art and architecture can at present be better known from Byzantine buildings and mosaics than from the available fragments of original work. The late Greek element of sixth-century art should be emphasized, not as evidence of revival, but rather of the tenacity and continuity of Greek culture. A parallel exists in the growth of early Christianity itself, in which Greek thought and energies became involved with ever-increasing effect. See N. H. Baynes, *The Hellenistic Civilization and East Rome*, Oxford, 1946. An English translation of D. Ainalov's important *Hellenistic Bases of Byzantine Art*, originally Russian, has been published.

30. W. S. George, *The Church of Saint Eirene at Constantinople*, Oxford, 1913. For Philippi, P. Lemerle, *Philippes et la Macédoine orientale*, 2 vols., Paris, 1945; for Kasr-ibn-Wardan, see H. C. Butler, *op. cit.*

31. F. Miltner, *Ephesos, Stadt der Artemis und des Johannes*, Vienna, 1957, pp. 119 ff. For the relationship between the Holy Apostles and Venice, O. Demus, *The Church of San Marco in Venice*, Washington, 1960, pp. 55 ff. and pp. 90 ff. On the domed Romanesque churches of France, R. Phené Spiers, *Architecture East and West*, London, 1905, pp. 153 ff.

32. The standard history of the Empire is that of G. Ostrogorsky, *History of the Byzantine State*, trans. by J. Hussey, Oxford, 1956. N. H. Baynes's, *The Byzantine Empire*, Oxford, 1949, is a good survey.

33. C. Mango, *The Brazen House*, Copenhagen, 1959, reviews past studies of the palace.

34. For the Chrysotriclinos, see J. Ebersolt, *Le grand palais de Constantinople*, Paris, 1910, pp. 77 ff. For a discussion of the text concerning the Church of Our Lady of the Pharos, see R. J. H. Jenkins and C. Mango, "The Date and Significance of the Tenth Homily of Photius," *Dumbarton Oaks Papers*, IX and X, 1956, pp. 123 ff. Plate 67 shows Professor

Conant's interpretation of Photius' homily and evidence from extant churches.

35. G. Downey, *op. cit.*, R. Janin, *op. cit.*, N. H. Baynes and H. Moss, *op. cit.*; and E. A. Grosvenor, *Constantinople*, 2 vols., Boston, 1885.

36. There is a pioneer work of 1912: A. Van Millingen, *Byzantine Churches in Constantinople*, London. In 1956–1960, *Dumbarton Oaks Papers* carried reports of the work in Istanbul by the Byzantine Institute; they contain information about several of these churches. For conjectural restorations, some of which are reproduced here, see K. J. Conant, *Early Medieval Church Architecture*, Baltimore, 1942. One would wish the buildings were much more widely known, for they represent a style of the highest quality and importance.

37. D. Talbot Rice, "Excavations at Bodrum Camii 1930," *Byzantion*, VIII, 1933, pp. 151 ff.

38. P. A. Underwood, "Preliminary Reports on the Restoration of the Frescoes in the Kariye Camii," *Dumbarton Oaks Papers*, IX-XIII, 1956–1960.

39. S. Der Nersessian, *Armenia and the Byzantine Empire*, Cambridge, Mass., 1947, Chap. 3; D. R. Buxton, *Russian Medieval Architecture*, Cambridge, 1934, Part II.

40. U. Monneret de Villard, "Le chiese della Mesopotamia," *Orientalia cristiana analecta*, CXXVIII, 1940, and *La Nubia medievale*, 4 vols., Cairo, 1935–1957; S. Clarke, *Christian Antiquities in the Nile Valley*, Oxford, 1912; A. J. Butler, *The Ancient Coptic Churches of Egypt*, 2 vols., Oxford, 1884; D. R. Buxton, "The Christian Antiquities of Northern Ethiopia ,"*Archaeologia*, XCII, 1947, pp. 1 ff.; J. Doresse, *Ethiopia*, New York, 1959.

41. For the Byzantine churches of Greece, see G. Millet, *L'école grecque dans l'architecture byzantine*, Paris, 1916; and, A. Frantz, "A Province of the Empire: Byzantine Churches in Greece," *Archaeology*, V, 1952, pp. 236 ff. For the mosaics of Stiris and Daphni, E. Diez and O. Demus, *Byzantine Mosaics in Greece*, Cambridge, Mass., 1931. For the visual

and iconographical principles of the decoration, O. Demus, *Byzantine Mosaic Decoration*, London, 1947, and "The Methods of the Byzantine Artist," *The Mint*, II, 1948, pp. 64 ff.

42. The Salonica monuments are inadequately published, but there is C. Diehl and others, *Les monuments chrétiens de Salonique*, Paris, 1918.

43. F. W. Hasluck, *Athos and Its Monasteries*, London, 1924; G. Millet, *Monuments byzantins de Mistra*, Paris, 1910; M. G. Soteriou, *Mistra*, Athens, 1956. For medieval buildings in Athens, M. Chatzidakis, *Athènes byzantines*, Athens, ca. 1955.

44. G. Millet, *L'ancien art serbe: Les églises*, Paris, 1919. The best illustrations are in A. Deroko, *Monumental and Decorative Architecture in Medieval Serbia*, Belgrade, 1953 (Serbo-Croat, with English summary and list of illustrations).

45. See G. H. Hamilton, *The Art and Architecture of Russia*, Pelican Books, 1954, Chap. 1-4 and 14-16. There is comparative material in K. J. Conant, "Novgorod, Constantinople and Kiev in Old Russian Church Architecture," *The Slavonic and East European Review*, XXII, 1944, pp. 75 ff.

46. C. Cecchelli, "Sguardo generale all'architettura bizantina in Italia," *Studi bizantini e neoellenici*, IV, 1935, pp. 1 ff. For San Marco, see O. Demus, *San Marco, op. cit.*

47. See Phené Spiers, *op. cit.*

48. P. Orsi, *Le chiese basiliane della Calabria*, Florence, 1929, pp. 7 ff.

49. A survey of Sicilian churches is given by J. A. Hamilton, *Byzantine Architecture and Decoration*, 2d ed., London, 1956, pp. 241 ff.

50. A. A. Vasiliev, *History of the Byzantine Empire*, Madison, 1952, pp. 650 ff.

51. For the domed mosques of Istanbul, C. Gurlitt, *Die Baukunst Konstantinopels*, 2 vols., Berlin, 1907–1912; and M. A. Charles, "Hagia Sophia and the Great Imperial Mosques," *Art Bulletin*, XII, 1930, pp. 321 ff., U. Vogt-Göknil, well illustrated, *Les mosquées turques*, Zurich, 1953. A recent monograph on Sinan: E. Egli, *Sinan*, Zurich, 1954.

SELECTED BIBLIOGRAPHY

There are many useful books and articles in addition to those cited in the notes. Though there is at present no general work of the first quality, a volume is promised in the Pelican History of Art series from Professor R. Krautheimer, a pre-eminent authority. For early Christian architecture there is E. C. Davies, *The Origins and Development of Early Christian Church Architecture*, London, 1952, a brief treatment; J. A. Hamilton, *Byzantine Architecture and Decoration*, 2d ed., London, 1956, largely descriptive. There are two older works which include much more material: O. Wulff, *Altchristliche und Byzantinische Kunst*, 2 vols., Berlin, 1918, and C. Diehl, *Manuel d'art byzantin*, 2d ed., 2 vols., Paris, 1925–1926.

Further works on particular aspects of the subject are R.

Krautheimer, *Corpus basilicarum christianarum Romae*, Rome, begun in 1937 and in progress in both Italian and English editions; A. Choisy, *L'art de bâtir chez les byzantins*, Paris, 1883, to be used gingerly; L. de Beylié, *L'habitation byzantine*, Paris, 1902, like Choisy, out of date but not replaced; J. Ebersolt, *Monuments d'architecture byzantine*, Paris, 1934.

A. Grabar, *Martyrium*, Paris, 3 vols., 1943–1946, discusses the origins and meaning of early Christian and early Byzantine architecture; the argument is sketched in part in his "Christian Architecture East and West," *Archaeology*, II, 1949, pp. 95 ff. Two articles by R. Krautheimer, "The Beginnings of Early Christian Architecture," *Review of Religions*, Jan., 1939, pp. 127 ff., and "Introduction to an 'Iconography' of Medieval Architecture," *Journal of the Warburg and Courtauld Institutes*, V, 1942, pp. 1 ff., are fundamental. P. A. Michelis, *An Aesthetic Approach to Byzantine Art*, London, 1955, contains provocative ideas.

Two very useful works of reference are F. L. Cross, ed., *The Oxford Dictionary of the Christian Church*, London, 1957, and F. van der Meer, *Atlas of the Early Christian World*, London, 1958; the latter is profusely illustrated. Liturgical, sacramental, and many other questions can often be answered by referring to F. Cabrol and H. Leclercq, *Dictionnaire d'archéologie chrétienne et de liturgie*, 15 vols., 1907–1953.

For related arts, O. M. Dalton, *Byzantine Art and Archaeology*, Oxford, 1911, is richer than his *East Christian Art*, Oxford, 1925. For early Christian art there is W. F. Volbach, *Frühchristliche Kunst*, Munich, 1958, splendidly illustrated. The later period is illustrated in D. Talbot Rice, *The Art of Byzantium*, London, 1959. Mosaics and frescoes after the fourth century are illustrated and discussed by A. Grabar, *Byzantine Painting*, Geneva, 1953.

The history of the early Church is detailed in the first three volumes of A. Fliche and V. Martin, *Histoire de l'église;* they have appeared as six volumes in English *(The History of the Primitive Church*, 4 vols., London, 1942–1948, and *The Church in the Christian Roman Empire*, 2 vols., London 1949–1952)*, trans. by E. C. Messenger. The later Church is covered in subsequent volumes of the French edition. There is a study of high Byzantine culture by J. M. Hussey, *Church and Learning in the Byzantine Empire*, Oxford, 1937, and a collection of translations of important documents in E. Barker, *Social and Political Thought in Byzantium*, Oxford, 1957. Byzantine life is vividly portrayed by L. Bréhier, *La civilisation byzantine*, Paris, 1950.

INDEX

Numbers in regular roman type refer to text pages; *italic* figures refer to the plates.

123

SOURCES OF ILLUSTRATION

Alinari, Rome: 33, 35, 42, 77

Alinari-Anderson, Rome: 15, 43, 95, 96

Archaeology, I, 1948, drawings by Detweiler: 24a and b

Archives Photographiques Françaises, Paris: 97

G. Boškovic, Belgrade. Courtesy A. Deroko: 87

H. C. Butler, *Ancient Architecture in Syria* (Leyden, 1907–20): 61

H. C. Butler, *Early Churches in Syria* (Princeton, 1929): 62

D. R. Buxton, Cambridge, England (from E. Mâle, *The Early Churches of Rome*, tr. by D. R. Buxton, London, 1960): 32

A. Calderini, *La Basilica di S. Lorenzo Maggiore in Milano* (Milan, 1951): 37

Courtesy Prof. K. J. Conant, Chevy Chase, Md.: 9, 10, 12, 19, 21, 67, 90

J. W. Crowfoot, *Early Churches in Palestine* (London, 1941): 8, 11

J. W. Crowfoot, "Churches at Jerash," *A Preliminary Report on the Joint Yale-British School of Archaeology Expedition to Jerusalem*, Supplementary Papers III (London, 1931). Plan, courtesy of Dr. C. S. Fisher: 23

G. Dehio and G. v. Bezold, *Die kirchliche Baukunst des Abendlandes* (Stuttgart, 1887–1901): 39

S. Der Nersessian, *Armenia and the Byzantine Empire* (Cambridge, Mass., 1947): 74

John Donat, London: 75, 76

J. Ebersolt, *Les églises de Constantinople* (Paris, 1913): 47

Fotocielo, Rome: 40, 65

Fototeca Unione, Rome: 31

Alison Frantz, Athens: 80

German Archaeological Institute, Rome: 16

Courtesy of the Royal Greek Embassy, Washington, D.C.: 82

G. H. Hamilton, *The Art and Architecture of Russia* (London, 1954): 89

J. A. Hamilton, *Byzantine Architecture and Decoration* (London, 1956): 79

H. Hell, *Istanbul* (Ernst Wasmuth Verlag, Tübingen, Germany): 46, 49, 59, 72

Hirmer Verlag, Munich: 27, 28, 48

Dr. Spiro K. Kostof, New Haven: 36

Krischen, F., *Die Landmauer von Konstantinopel*, (Berlin, 1938): 17

Lemerle, A., *Philippes... II*, (Paris, 1946): 63

Dr. William MacDonald, New Haven: 1, 2, 6, 20, 22, 29, 30, 34, 41, 50, 51, 52, 54, 55, 56, 57, 58, 60, 71, 78, 84, 94, 98, 99

Miltner, F., *Ephesos*, (Vienna, 1958): 64

National Museum of Belgrade. Photo courtesy A. Deroko: 86, 88

Courtesy of the Opera di San Marco, Venice: 93

N. Pevsner, *Europäische Architektur* (Munich, 1957): 13

D. S. Robertson, *A Handbook of Greek and Roman Architecture* (Cambridge, England, 1943): 4

A. M. Schneider, *Byzanz* (Berlin, 1936): 44

The Society for Cultural Relations with the U.S.S.R., London: 92

Dr. Michael Stettler, Bern: 14

Cecil Stewart, *Byzantine Legacy* (London, George, Allen & Unwin, 1947): 85

Cecil Stewart, *Early Christian, Byzantine and Romanesque Architecture* (London, Longmans Green & Co., 1954): 5, 45, 81

Swift, E. H., *Hagia Sophia* (New York, 1940): 53

Paul Underwood, Byzantine Institute, Washington, D.C.: 73

Verzone, P., *Alahan Monastir* (Turin, 1956): 26

A. Vogt, *Le Livre des Cérémonies* (Paris, 1935): 66

M. de Vogüé, *Architecture Civile et Religieuse du Ier au VIIe Siècle* (Paris, 1865): 18

M. de Vogüé, *La Syrie Centrale* (Paris, 1865–77): 25

J. B. Ward-Perkins, "The Italian Element in Late Roman and Early Medieval Architecture," *Proceedings of the British Academy*, XXXIII, 1947: 38

O. Wulff, *Altchristliche und Byzantinische Kunst* (Berlin, 1918): 83

Courtesy of Yale University, School of Fine Arts, New Haven: 3, 7, 68, 69, 70, 91, 100